Adults

Kieran Hurley

methuen | drama

LONDON · NEW YORK · OXFORD · NEW DELHI · SYDNEY

METHUEN DRAMA
Bloomsbury Publishing Plc
50 Bedford Square, London, WC1B 3DP, UK
1385 Broadway, New York, NY 10018, USA
29 Earlsfort Terrace, Dublin 2, Ireland

BLOOMSBURY, METHUEN DRAMA and the Methuen
Drama logo are trademarks of Bloomsbury Publishing Plc

First published in Great Britain 2023

A catalogue record for this book is available from the British Library.

A catalog record for this book is available from the Library of Congress.

ISBN: PB: 978-1-3504-4029-6
ePDF: 978-1-3504-4030-2
eBook: 978-1-3504-4031-9

Series: Modern Plays

Typeset by Mark Heslington Ltd, Scarborough, North Yorkshire

To find out more about our authors and books visit
www.bloomsbury.com and sign up for our newsletters.

ADULTS

By Kieran Hurley

Cast

Conleth Hill	IAIN
Dani Heron	ZARA
Anders Hayward	JAY

Creative Team

Kieran Hurley	Writer
Roxana Silbert	Director
Anna Orton	Set & Costume Designer
Colin Grenfell	Lighting Designer
Calum Paterson	Sound Designer
Emily Jane Boyle	Movement Director
EmmaClaire Brightlyn	Fight Director

Production Team

Kevin McCallum	Head of Production
Renny Robertson	Head of Lighting & Sound
Dave Bailey	Lighting & Sound Technician
Fi Elliott	Lighting & Sound Technician
Jamie Hayes	Production Manager
Alma Lindenhovius	Stage Manager
Judy Stewart	Deputy Stage Manager

Kieran Hurley is a playwright from Edinburgh, Scotland. He started out making shows at the Arches in Glasgow, a now-defunct performance art venue and nightclub underneath the city's Central Station where he also worked in the cloakroom. He has since worked closely with the Traverse Theatre, the National Theatre of Scotland and others, with his plays being performed in multiple translations across the world. Recent theatre includes: *The Enemy* (National Theatre of Scotland); *Mouthpiece* (Traverse Theatre) and *Square Go* (co-written with Gary McNair, Francesca Moody Productions). His debut screenplay *Beats* was co-written with director Brian Welsh and adapted from his breakout play of the same name. With his partner and frequent collaborator Julia Taudevin, he is co-Artistic Director of the theatre company Disaster Plan. His *Plays 1* collected works is published by Methuen.

Roxana Silbert is a freelance theatre, audio and screen director who works mainly commissioning, developing, directing and producing new drama. She was Artistic Director of Hampstead Theatre (2019–22); Artistic Director of Birmingham Repertory Theatre (2013–19); Associate Director of the Royal Shakespeare Company (2009–13); Artistic Director of Paines Plough Theatre Company (2005–2009); Literary Director at the Traverse Theatre, Edinburgh (2001–2004); and Associate Director of the Royal Court (1998–2000). She has been instrumental in launching the careers of many writers who are now leading screen and theatre dramatists.

Theatre credits include: *Orphans* by Dennis Kelly (Birmingham Rep/Traverse Theatre/Paines Plough/Soho Theatre) for the Edinburgh Festival (Fringe First, Herald Angel awards); *Breakfast with Ravenhill* (Paines Plough/Traverse Theatre), pioneering breakfast theatre at the Edinburgh Festival (TMA Award, Fringe First and Spirit of the Fringe Awards); *Long Time Dead* by Rona Munro (Paines Plough/Traverse Theatre/Plymouth Theatre Royal/Soho Theatre) for Edinburgh Festival (Stage Award, The Independent Award, TMA Awards nominee); *Strawberries in January* by Evelyne de la Chenlière (Paines Plough/Traverse Theatre) for the Edinburgh Festival; *After the End* by Dennis Kelly (Paines Plough/Bush Theatre/Traverse Theatre/59E59 New York/national and international tour) for Edinburgh Festival; *Iron* by Rona Munro (Traverse Theatre/Royal Court) for Edinburgh Festival (The Stage Award, Evening Standard Award, John Whiting Award); *The Slab Boys* and *Still Life* by John Byrne, Traverse Theatre and national number 1 tour; *The People Next Door* by Henry Adam (Traverse

Theatre/Theatre Royal Stratford) and then international tour and 59E59 New York for Edinburgh Festival (Fringe First, Glasgow Herald Award, Time Out Award, Critics Circle Awards); *Green Field* by Riccardo Galgani (Traverse Theatre); *Quartz* by Catherine Czerkawska (Traverse Theatre).

Anna Orton is a designer working across theatre, dance, opera and exhibition. Her previous work exhibiting, performing and curating as a visual artist in some of Scotland's most pioneering spaces continues to influence her work in performance design.

Her recent work includes the multi-award-winning production of Handel's *Messiah* directed by Tom Morris, which premiered at Bristol Old Vic and was followed by a national cinema and online streaming release. Other designs include *Kidnapped* (National Theatre of Scotland), *This Is Memorial Device* (Royal Lyceum Edinburgh), *Robin Hood Legend of the Forgotten Forest* and *King Lear* (Bristol Old Vic), *La Bohème* (Scottish Opera), *A Christmas Carol* (Pitlochry Festival Theatre – Shortlisted for *Best Emerging Designer*, World Stage Design Awards 2021) and *Welcome Home* (Soho Theatre). She has designed for many prestigious companies including Live Theatre Newcastle, English Touring Opera, Buxton Opera Festival and the Watermill Theatre amongst others.

Colin Grenfell is a lighting designer whose work includes: *Pride and Prejudice* (*sort of)* (Criterion Theatre); *Educating Rita, Oh When The Saints* (Perth Theatre); *The Time Machine* (Original Theatre); *Cinderella* (Dundee Rep Theatre); *Leopards* (Rose Theatre); *This is Paradise, Still, The Devil Masters, Pandas, On the Exhale* (Traverse); *Christmas Dinner* (Royal Lyceum Edinburgh); *The King of Hell's Palace* (Hampstead Theatre); *Gypsy, Macbeth, The Cherry Orchard, Kes* (Royal Exchange Theatre, Manchester); *Black Watch, 365, Men Should Weep, The Bacchae, Granite* (National Theatre of Scotland); *Tao of Glass* (Manchester International Festival); *An Improbable Musical, Still No Idea, 70 Hill Lane, Coma, The Paper Man, Spirit* (Improbable); *A Christmas Carol* (Everyman Liverpool, Spymonkey); *Tamburlaine* (RSC); *The Mentor* (Theatre Royal Bath & Vaudeville Theatre); *Lost Without Words, Lifegame, Theatre of Blood* (Improbable/Royal National Theatre); *The Village Social* (National Theatre of Wales); *Beauty and the Beast* (MCA, Chicago, Abrons New York, Adelaide Festival); *The Caretaker* (Liverpool Everyman, Trafalgar

Studios, BAM); *A Midsummer Night's Dream, Half Life, The Mother, Forever Yours, Marie-Lou, Wild Goose Dreams, Xmas Eve* (Theatre Royal Bath); *Cat on a Hot Tin Roof* (Theatr Clwyd, Best Lighting Award at the 2017 Wales Theatre Awards); *The Elephant Man* (Best Design CATS award); *The Hanging Man* (Best Design TMA awards).

Calum Paterson is a sound designer and composer. He specialises in immersive and binaural techniques, and creates work in all areas of live performance and digital media. From audio-drama to theatre, Calum is passionate about using sound and music to tell transformative stories that bring people and communities together through collective experience. Calum is the Creative Director of The Audio Story Company, an arts organisation who produce immersive-audio experiences.

Live performance credits include: *Castle Lennox, Life is a Dream, Wendy & Peter Pan, Mrs Puntila and Her Man Matti, Pride & Prejudice* (*sort of), The Hour We Knew Nothing of Each Other* (Royal Lyceum Edinburgh); *Me and My Sister Tell Each Other Everything, Food of Love, If You're Feeling Sinister* (Tron Theatre); *The Dodo Experiment* (Citizens Theatre); *Message from the Skies* (Edinburgh's Hogmanay 2022); *The Cheviot, the Stag and the Black, Black Oil, The 306: Day* (National Theatre of Scotland); *SPRING!* (Scottish Ballet); *Stand By* (Utter Theatre); *Ceilidh* (Theatre Gu Leor); *Happiness Collectors, Merry* (The Audio Story Co.).

Digital and screen credits include: *The Woolgatherers, The Lost Reindeer* (The Audio Story Co.); *CreateWorks* (Braw Fox Theatre and Edinburgh University); *Happy Ark Day* (National Theatre of Scotland, BBC Scotland); *The Unseen Child* (Hopscotch Theatre Co.).

Emily Jane Boyle is a movement director whose theatre credits include: *Leopoldstadt* (West End/Broadway – Olivier Award for Best New Play, Tony Award for Best Play); *Pride and Prejudice* (*sort of)* (Tron Theatre/West End/UK tour – Olivier Award for Best Comedy); *Charlie and the Chocolate Factory, Sunshine on Leith* (UK tours); *Wilf* (Traverse Theatre); *Macbeth (an undoing), Jumpy, The Lion, the Witch and the Wardrobe, Hedda Gabler* (Royal Lyceum Edinburgh); *Exit the King* (National Theatre); *Henry VI, The Mirror and the Light* (Royal Shakespeare Company); *Kidnapped, How to Act* (National Theatre of Scotland); *Measure For Measure* (Globe Theatre); *Oresteia: This Restless House, Lanark* (Citizens Theatre/EIF); *Trainspotting, Cuttin' A*

Rug (Citizens Theatre); *Nora: A Doll's House* (Citizens Theatre/Young Vic); *Muster Station: Leith* (Grid Iron); *Richard III* (Leeds Playhouse); *Talent* (Sheffield Crucible); *Habeas Corpus* (Menier); *A Midsummer Night's Dream* (Regent's Park); *The Return, Not About Heroes* (Eden Court); *Still Game: Live* (SECC Hydro); *The Red Balloon* (National Youth Ballet); *The Cook, The Thief, His Wife and Her Lover* (Faena Theatre); *Tay Bridge, Passing Places, Great Expectations* and *The Cheviot, the Stag and the Black, Black Oil* (Dundee Rep).

Television and film credits include: *The Crown* (Netflix); *Our Ladies* (Sony); *Two Doors Down* (BBC); *In Plain Sight* (ITV); *God Help the Girl* (Barry Mendel/Sigma); Glasgow Commonwealth Games Opening and Closing Ceremonies (BBC).

Conleth Hill is an Olivier award-winning actor and theatre director, known internationally for his portrayal of Lord Varys in smash-hit TV series *Game of Thrones*. He returns to the Traverse stage twenty-five years after his first performance on its stages, having starred in Communicado's *The Suicide* by Nikolai Erdman, as well as *Stones in his Pockets*. He has won Olivier Awards for Best Actor for his roles in both *The Producers* (West End) and *Stones in his Pockets* (West End/Broadway), and has been nominated for a Tony Award twice, for *Stones in his Pockets* and *The Seafarer*.

Theatre credits include: the Olivier-nominated West End production of *Who's Afraid of Virginia Woolf* and *Macbeth* (Berkeley Rep) alongside Frances McDormand, *Philistines, All's Well That Ends Well, The White Guard* and *The Cherry Orchard* (National Theatre); *Quartermaine's Terms* (Wyndham's Theatre) and *Dallas Sweetman* (Canterbury Festival), directed by Roxana Silbert.

Television credits include: *Undoing Martin Parker* (BBC); *Holding* (ITV) based on Graham Norton's novel; *Dublin Murders* (BBC/Starz); *Hang Ups* (C4); a much-loved turn as Elsie in Peter Kay's *Car Share* (BBC); *Magpie Murders* (BBC) and *The Lovers* (Sky).

Film credits include: *Salmon Fishing in the Yemen* alongside Ewan McGregor; Woody Allen's *Whatever Works*; political drama *Official Secrets* and Claire Dunne's critically acclaimed drama *Herself*.

Dani Heron trained at the London Academy of Music and Dramatic Art (LAMDA).

Theatre credits include: *Sugar Coat* (Southwark Playhouse, London); *Cinderella* (PACE Theatre, Paisley); *Underwood Lane* (Tron Theatre, Glasgow); *The Golden Rage*; *Ten Things To Do Before You Die*; *My Name is Sarah and...* (A Play, A Pie and A Pint); *Sugar Coat* (Vault Festival, London); *Peter Gynt* (National Theatre/Edinburgh Festival Theatre); *Rebus: Long Shadows* (Birmingham Rep, National tour); *Immaculate Correction* (King's Head Theatre, London); *Long Day's Journey into Night* (Citizens Theatre Glasgow/Home Manchester); *306: Day* (National Theatre of Scotland); *Jumpy* (Royal Lyceum Edinburgh); *The James Plays* (National Theatre of Scotland); *The Venetian Twins* (Royal Lyceum Edinburgh); *A Perfect Stroke* (Òran Mór/Traverse Theatre); *Chariots of Fire* (West End)

Television credits include: *Crime* (Britbox); *Murder Island* (Channel 4); *Casualty* (BBC); *Armchair Detectives* (BBC).

Film credits include: *Skin Deep*; *I Am Me*; *Rat Trap*.

Anders Hayward is the star of the widely acclaimed third season of *Guilt* (BBC), opposite Mark Bonnar. He also played the lead in E4/Hulu comedy-drama *Gap Year* and featured in John Crowley's adaptation of *Life After Life* (BBC).

Film credits include: Scott Graham's *Run* opposite Mark Stanley, which premiered at the Tribeca Film Festival, *Looted* directed by Rene Pannevis, and Johnny Barrington's upcoming directorial debut *Silent Roar*.

TRAVERSE THEATRE

Here we are – together – marking sixty years of the Traverse. Together, we celebrate six decades of stories that connect, inspire, challenge, entertain and that contribute to the cultural voice of our nation. With an abundance of shows from talented artists with urgent stories that bring life and vitality to our stages – both in-person and digital – the Traverse continues to be a platform for debate, a space for our community, and home of memorable experiences. Across our programme, you can encounter trailblazing creativity that offers unique opportunities to explore the world around us, connect with the lives of others and that spark that vital curiosity in what it is to be human.

The Traverse is a champion of performance, experience and discovery. Enabling people to access and engage with theatre is our fundamental mission, and we want our work to represent, speak to and be seen by the broadest cross section of society. We are specialists in revealing untold perspectives in innovative ways. This is our role as Scotland's premier new work theatre and a commitment that drives each strand of our work.

Our year-round programme bursts with new stories, live and digital performances that challenge, inform and entertain our audiences. We empower artists and audiences to make sense of the world today, providing a safe space to question, learn, empathise and – crucially – encounter different people and experiences. Conversation and the coming together of groups are central to a democratic society, and we champion equal expression and understanding for the future of a healthy national and international community.

The Traverse would not exist without our overarching passion for developing new stories and embracing the unexplored. We work with bold voices and raw talent – with an emphasis on the Scottish-based – to create the art, artists, and performances that can be seen on our platforms year-round. We invest in ideas and support individuals to push boundaries by placing them at the centre of their own practice, and through artist-led and co-created projects like Class Act and

Street Soccer: #SameTeam, we create spaces for stories to take form and grow.

We aim for the timely stories and creative programmes that start life with us to have a global impact, through tours, co-productions, digital life, and translations. We are critically acclaimed and recognised the world over for our originality and artistic risk, which we hope will create some of the most talked-about plays, productions, directors, writers, and actors for years to come.

The Traverse's commitment to bringing new and bold storytelling to global audiences is amplified in Edinburgh each August, when international audiences make the Traverse programme – often referred to as the 'beating heart of the Fringe' – their first port of call in a city overflowing with entertainment offerings.

Here's to the Traverse and all who have created with, played for, visited, and continue to champion everything we are. Our past successes drive our present and future direction, in the knowledge that our unique ability to nurture new talent and engage audiences through ambitious storytelling has never been more crucial in creating and sustaining a vibrant theatre landscape that reflects and challenges the world today.

Find out more about our work: traverse.co.uk

With Thanks

The Traverse extends grateful thanks to all of its supporters, including those who prefer to remain anonymous. Their valuable contributions ensure that the Traverse continues to champion stories and storytellers in all of its forms, help develop the next generation of creative talent and lead vital projects in our local community, Scotland and beyond.

With your help, we can write the next scene of our story.

Visit traverse.co.uk/support-us to find out more.

Individual Supporters

Diamond
Alan & Penny Barr
Katie Bradford
Kirsten Lamb
David Rodgers

Platinum
Judy & Steve
Angus McLeod
Iain Millar
Mike & Carol Ramsay

Gold
Roger & Angela Allen
Carola Bronte-Stewart
Iona Hamilton

Silver
Bridget M Stevens
Allan Wilson
Gaby Thomson
Chris & Susan Gifford
Lesley Preston
John Healy

Bronze
Barbara Cartwright
Alex Oliver & Duncan Stephen
Patricia Pugh
Beth Thomson
Julia & David Wilson
Stephanie & Neil
Drs Urzula & Michael Glienecke
Viv Phillips
Jon Best & Kate Duffield

Trusts, Foundations and Grants
Anderson Anderson & Brown Charitable Initiative
Arnold Clark Community Fund
Backstage Trust
Baillie Gifford Community Awards
British Council Scotland and Creative Scotland: UK in Japan 2019–20
Bruce Wake Charitable Trust
Cruden Foundation
D'Oyly Carte Charitable Trust

Adapt and Thrive, part of the Scottish Government's Community and Third Sector Recovery Programme and delivered in partnership by Firstport, Corra Foundation, SCVO, Just Enterprise, Community Enterprise and Social Investment Scotland.

In Residence Partners
The Traverse has the support of the Peggy Ramsay Foundation/Film 4 Playwrights Awards Scheme.

The Traverse Theatre is further supported by IASH, the Institute of Advanced Research in the Humanities, the University of Edinburgh.

Challenge Project
Traverse Theatre is currently participating in Creative Informatics' Challenge project as one of the Challenge Holders.

Creative Creative Informatics supports individuals and organisations working across the creative industries in Edinburgh and South East Scotland to develop new products, services and businesses using data and data-driven technologies. The programme is delivered by the University of Edinburgh, in partnership with Edinburgh Napier University, CodeBase and Creative Edinburgh.

Creative Informatics is funded by the Creative Industries Clusters Programme managed by the Arts & Humanities Research Council with additional support from the Scottish Funding Council. It is also part of the City Region Deal Data-Driven Innovation initiative.

Adults

Scene

A very small one-bedroom flat, somewhere in Edinburgh.

Characters

Iain, *sixties*
Zara, *thirties*
Jay, *thirties*

A dash at the end of a line of dialogue indicates that the next line cuts in quickly before the line has a chance to complete.

The script calls for full nudity, though this may be altered in line with the needs of production if necessary. If so, the characters should nevertheless be almost entirely naked.

Snap, lights up. In the millisecond that lights snap up, a scream, a shocking splash of pink –

Zara Argh!

Iain Jesus! Christ!

Iain *stands, stunned; head, shoulders and chest dripping in thick, creamy, pink gloop.* **Zara** *stands facing him, a now empty bottle of strawberry flavoured Yazoo yoghurt drink in her hand.*

Zara How the fuck did you get in here?

Iain It, it was on the latch, I, I –

Zara How'd you get in to the fucking building?

Iain The door downstairs was open –

Zara Those wankers! Oh my God I'm sorry!

Iain I, I, I –

Zara I'm really sorry!

Iain I mean! Really!

They are in the bedroom of a small Edinburgh tenement flat; the compact, well-maintained private sanctuary of a young woman. A neatly made bed. A chest of drawers with a couple of framed family photos on top of it. A small IKEA chair, perhaps. A glass bottle filled with fairy lights. A kimono hanging off the back of a door that leads to the hallway. Another door leading to a tiny bathroom.

Zara You gave me a fright.

Iain I was just standing!

Zara Here. Here.

She hands him a negligee, he wipes his face with it. She recognises him.

Zara Oh holy shit.

Iain What? What?

Zara   Oh, nothing.

Iain   This is a bloody new jacket!

Zara, *flustered, starts trying to help him mop himself up.*

Zara   You're early!

Iain   Am I?

Zara   Yes!

Iain   No I'm not.

Zara   You're supposed to wait.

Iain   I, I, I didn't want to be seen.

Zara   You're not supposed to fucking –

Iain   Sorry. I've never been here before, to this sort of, I don't –

Zara   Right.

Iain   I'm not scary.

Zara   I really am sorry about the jacket.

Iain   It's buggered, isn't it?

Zara   We have, uh, spares.

Iain   Spares?

Zara   Some spare clothes. Not much, but some.

Iain   What like, t-shirts? I don't really wear t-shirts.

Zara   What size are you?

Iain   Large.

Beat.

Extra large.

Beat.

They've not been left here have they? By other . . . blokes?

Zara *pulls out a garish yellow shirt.* **Iain** *looks at it, unimpressed.*

Iain   No.

Zara   Maybe it'll suit you.

Zara *hands him the shirt. He stares at it.*

There's a bathroom over there, if you'd like to make your way over this way please, you can wash up and get changed.

Iain *reluctantly takes the shirt. He heads to the bathroom.*

Zara   Take your time.

Iain *exits through the bathroom door and closes it behind him.*

Zara   Fuck, fuck, fuck.

She tries making a phone call. No answer. She records a voice note, hushed but urgent.

Zara   Where the fuck are you? He's here. He's here and he's – he's my old fucking teacher. Like an actual – one who actually knew me. He's not recognised me. You better get here before he bolts, because you can't afford to –

Noises off from the bathroom.

Zara   Look, just get your arse up here, will you? For fuck's sake! Fuck!

Iain *meekly peers round the door, in a too-big bright yellow shirt. He looks ridiculous, like a giant lemon. He stands like this, stock still, until* **Zara** *sees him.*

Zara   Oh! Hi! You look – fantastic.

Zara *turns and instantly busies herself with mopping up the spilt yoghurt drink.*

Iain   I look absurd.

Zara   Please, take a seat. Make yourself comfortable.

Iain   It makes me look like a giant peanut M&M. Only one that drinks Carling.

She desperately tries to maintain a professional air while cleaning up.

Zara   Well I think you look ten years younger.

Iain   You're just saying that.

A pause. **Iain** *stands, awkward, uncertain what to do, as* **Zara** *mops up.*

Iain   The um, the advert said – for, for a man. A chap. A sort of a – fella, you see.

Zara   Yes. He's on his way. If you don't mind just leaving the payment on the dresser there, please, thank you.

Iain   Oh, oh yes. Of course.

Iain *produces an envelope of cash, places it nervously on the dresser.* **Zara** *takes it, counts the cash as she talks.*

Iain   So . . . I just, wait. Do I?

Zara   Yes.

Iain   Like at the dentist?

Zara   I suppose so. Yes. Please, do take a seat. And, shoes off please.

Iain   Excuse me?

Zara   I'd normally ask you to take your shoes off when you come in, but there was a lot going on, so if you don't mind –

Iain   Right.

Iain *takes his shoes off.* **Zara** *takes them from him.* **Iain** *sits on a chair, nervous, as* **Zara** *continues to fuss around the space. She smooths down the bedsheets, moving with swift expert familiarity, like a hotel worker.*

Iain   What are you doing?

Zara   I'm . . . preparing. The space.

Iain   Right.

Zara   Sorry. It should really have been set up for you before you arrive.

Zara *continues tidying away the objects of her private life. Kimono into the cupboard, hairbrush and make-up bag swiftly into a drawer, and so on.*

Iain   So you, uh, you're one of the um, ladies of the uh . . . you work here too then, I suppose?

Zara   Uh huh. That's right.

Iain   I didn't mean to frighten you.

Zara   Please, it's fine.

Iain   I don't want to frighten anyone. I'm not a scary man.

Zara   It was my fault, okay? It's fine.

Iain   I imagine that sort of thing happens all the time.

Zara   Um . . .

Iain   No. No, probably not.

Zara *tosses a throw over the bed. It folds over itself. She tuts and tries again.* **Iain** *instinctively takes a corner.*

Zara   Oh, okay –

They lay the throw over the bed, **Zara** *tidies it just so.*

Zara   Thank you.

Iain *takes out a hip flask and reaches it to his lips.*

Zara   Oh, I'm sorry but you can't do that here.

He looks at her.

Iain   What?

Zara   There's no drinking, sorry. It's a safety policy. You're nervous, that's okay. But you –

Iain   I'm not nervous! I'm fine!

Zara   I can get you a glass of water of you like.

Iain   Whoop-de-doo.

Zara   I can take it from you, if it helps –

Zara *goes to take the flask.* **Iain** *pulls it away from her.*

Iain   No! I am not a child okay, I'm not a –

Zara   That's okay. Let's all stay calm –

Iain   I'm calm!

Zara   So just give me the flask.

Iain   First you assault me –

Zara   It was hardly assault, if you could just give it here then –

Iain   No! You assaulted me with a, with a –

Zara   Strawberry Yazoo. And –

Iain   With a strawberry Yazoo. And now I'm the one being accused of being some kind of menace, or –

Zara   Please. I'm sorry I've upset you –

Zara *takes the flask.*

Iain   Whatever happened to 'the customer is always right', eh? The disrespect of –

Iain *snatches the flask back.*

Zara   Please! Mr Urquhart, I –

Zara *puts her hand to her mouth. Beat.*

Iain   How do you know I'm Urquhart?

Zara   Ah shite.

Iain   How do you know I'm Urquhart?

Zara   Of course I know you're Mr Urquhart. Sir.

Beat.

Zara   You don't recognise me. That's fine.

Beat.

Zara   Zara Harvey. Sixth year school leavers 2009.

Iain   Oh.

Zara   Kevin and Rebecca's daughter?

Iain   Oh Jesus. Oh Jesus Christ.

Zara   Good afternoon, Mr Urquhart.

Iain   Zara. You, um. You look. You look, diff . . . I never expected to . . .

Zara   It's all the make-up probably, it's fine.

Iain   I, I – lots of young people pass through my um . . .

Zara   It's fine. You're fine.

Iain   Oh, oh, oh bloody, bloody hell. Please. Please, please, you cannot tell, promise me you won't tell anyone that I –

Zara   I don't tell.

Iain   It's really the first time that I've ever even thought about coming to a place like –

Zara   It's okay. I'll promise not to tell anyone you're paying for sex, and you'll promise not to tell anyone I'm selling it. And you'll start respecting my rules. Deal?

She takes the hip flask from his stunned hand.

Zara   You can get it back at the end. Okay?

Iain   You won't go Twittering about this or anything?

Zara   I don't – what? No.

Iain   Right.

Zara   It's okay.

Iain   Okay.

Zara   You're okay.

Iain   Right. Okay. Okay, right.

Pause. Suddenly **Iain** *makes directly for the exit door.*

Zara   Mr Urquhart?

Iain   I'm going. Thank you, Zara. I'm leaving now.

Zara   What? No.

Iain   I have made a grave error in coming here.

Zara   He's coming over already, he's on his way.

Iain   This has been a terrible lapse in judgement. Completely out of character. And I hope that you will try to never think of it again – where are my shoes?

Zara   Please, he doesn't usually work today, I've called him over special. Look. I'll call him.

Zara *stands between* **Iain** *and the door, phone in hand.*

Zara   See where he is. Okay?

She calls. No answer. She hangs up.

Iain   I'm going.

Zara   Please, Iain. Don't leave. You've paid already.

Iain   Where did you put my shoes?

Zara   Look, Iain. Iain. If you didn't want this, you wouldn't have come. Nobody is judging you. I see you. I do.

Iain   I came here because I wanted to, to, to –

Zara   I know. I know.

Iain   – to see if I, I . . .

Zara   I know. It's okay.

Iain   But now you're here.

Zara   Yes.

Iain   And it's different.

Zara   You're alright. Come here, sit down.

She guides him, expertly back into his seat. He sits.

It's okay. Here. See? It's fine. This is fine.

She massages his shoulders, trying to calm him. It's awkward and desperate, but something in what she's doing or saying works.

He'll be here really, really soon. Don't you want to stay? Just to see?

Beat.

Relax.

Beat.

Iain   Can I please, please, please, have a drink? Please.

Beat.

Zara   Okay then.

Iain   Oh, thank Christ.

Zara   One drink.

Zara *hands him the hip flask.* **Iain** *necks a big glug. Then another. Pause. He exhales.* **Zara** *holds her hand out. He gives her the flask.*

Iain   Bloody fucking hell.

Zara   Yup.

Iain   Zara Harvey.

Zara   Uh huh.

Iain   What on earth is a girl like you doing in a place like this?

Zara   Well. I might suggest that's a little bit of a bold question for you to ask right now, given the circumstances.

Beat.

Relax. You're not the first ex-teacher I've had come in here you know.

Iain   Really?

Zara   There's one comes in regular. Delighted with the discovery, so he was. Jackpot. He bought me a school uniform, for when he comes. It's one of the actual school uniforms, got the badge on it and everything.

Iain   That's, that's reprehensible. That's disgusting.

Zara   I can show you it if you like, he keeps it here –

Iain   No! I am not like that, I am not a pervert!

Zara   Suit yourself.

Beat.

Iain   Would you mind telling me . . . who?

Zara   You'll be reassured to know I won't say.

Iain   Right. I bet you I know who it is though.

Zara   You'd be surprised. Let's just say Edinburgh is very small. And everyone is a pervert.

She continues setting up the space. Putting away photographs that hang on walls, and so on.

Iain   Look, I, I really don't want you to think that . . . I'm honestly not like the other men that come in here you know.

Zara   You're exactly like the other men that come here.

Iain   I'm really not, I just –

Zara   Trust me. Almost all of the men who come here want me to know that they're not like any of the other men who come here. It is, ironically enough, the one thing you all have in common.

Iain   Well, I, I wanted a, it's different because I wanted to see a man you see –

Zara   A boy.

Iain   Excuse me?

Zara   You asked for a boy, that's what you said.

Iain   Well I didn't mean –

Zara   You wanted a nice young smooth guy, I know. It's okay, you're not alone. Lot's of people want that. There's no judgement here, sir. This is a safe, non-judgemental space. It's okay.

Pause.

Iain   How's . . . how's your dad?

Zara   Not so well, if I'm honest. Will I tell him you're asking for him?

Iain   I –

Zara   It's okay. I'm joking.

Iain   Right. Yes. Okay. And your mum?

Zara   She's dead.

Iain   Oh I'm very sorry.

Zara   It's fine. Well. It's what happens. You get older. And your parents die. She thought very highly of you, you know. Thought you were a very decent, honourable man.

Iain   That's very um . . . thank you. That's always humbling to hear. I'm sorry for your loss.

Zara   Cheers, I suppose.

Iain   Does he, does your dad uh, know about all this then . . .

Zara   Oh, fuck off please, sir.

Iain   Of course. Sorry.

Zara *resumes setting up the space.*

Zara   Are you dizzy? You've met my dad.

Iain   Yes. Right. And how long have you –

Zara   Few years. One way or another, depending on what you're including.

Iain   Shit.

Zara   What?

Iain   That's just – quite a long time to be lying to your dad.

Zara   I spend a lot of time looking after him by the way. This isn't the only thing I do with my life. And the flexibility is –

Iain   You were a very good student, you know.

Zara   Oh, here we go.

Iain   You had real potential, you really did.

Zara   I'm doing fine.

Iain   Are you still friends with any of those other girls, from your year?

Zara   No.

Beat.

Zara   I'm still in touch with one or two, maybe. On socials. I see updates on their lives sometimes.

Iain   And what do they think? Of your . . . life choices.

Zara   They think I'm writing a book.

Iain   And are you?

Zara   You're sounding a bit judgy if I'm honest, Iain. There's no judgement in this space, okay? This is a non-judgemental space, remember? I'm doing fine. Thank you.

Iain   It's just . . . haven't you ever thought about doing . . . something else? Something less –

Zara   What? Exploitative?

Iain   Yes.

Zara   We work as a collective. A workers' co-operative. Well a co-op of two, for now. We share the space. Share the contact number. Share the organisational responsibilities, share the profits.

Iain   I see.

Zara   No pimps, no wankers.

Iain   That's very, um, smart. And progressive.

Zara   Thank you. That, in fact, is our U.S.P. A lot of men want what we offer but feel . . . uncertain about it. We aim to reassure them – through our non-hierarchical business practice, our safer spaces policy, and our accepting and judgement-free approach to catering for a wide range of unusual preferences – that it's –

Iain   Ethical?

Zara   Yes.

Iain   And is it?

Zara   It's a job Iain. A business, even.

Iain   Do the neighbours not get . . . suspicious?

Zara   We don't have neighbours. It's all Airbnbs. Hardly anyone actually lives here lives here.

Iain   Right. But aren't you worried that someone could just – call the police? What would happen to you? If anyone did?

Zara   I'd like to talk about something else if you don't mind Iain. Let's catch up. How's Mrs Urquhart?

Iain   Ach.

Zara   Ah, I see. Well, you're not the first man to come in here after arguing with his wife, sir.

Iain   No. No, I suppose not.

Beat.

You have kids, Zara?

Zara   Nope, absolutely love to be asked about it though, thank you.

Iain   No, don't suppose you could. Well, just as well. Never, ever do. It's a living fucking nightmare. Destroys your life.

Zara   Uh huh.

Iain   It's fine when they're little. Mostly. You sort of think it's going to be like that forever. Reading. Stories and things. I loved that, that was the best part.

Zara   Okay, Iain. I can listen to all this if you want, this stuff. Really, I can. But I will have to start the clock.

Iain   What, for listening?

Zara   Yes. That is a lot of what I do. I'd have to start charging you.

Iain   People come here just to talk?

Zara   Never just that. But you'd be surprised how much of it is about feelings.

Iain   Wouldn't it be easier to just see a therapist?

Zara   No. For a lot of men, it really, really wouldn't.

Beat.

Iain   My favourite was Thomas. Old Thomas. Thomas the Tank. Loved it.

Zara   Do you want role play, is that it?

Iain   Sorry?

Zara I mean, that's all much more my wheelhouse, but we could discuss some options on his arrival – though it will cost you extra.

Iain Excuse me?

Zara We have a milkmaid costume, if you want him to dress as a little girl, or we could get you a crotchless train conductor, niche I know but sounds like it might be right up your street –

Iain What? No! That is absolutely revolting!

Zara Well actually, Thomas the Tank Engine is revolting. So there.

Iain What?

Zara It is. Pseudo-imperialist nostalgic colonial nonsense.

Iain Oh, come on.

Zara It espouses top-down leadership, everyone working to the command of the Fat Controller, whose authority is upheld by a kind of punitive justice system. Any deviant behaviour is severely disciplined, and punished – honestly, any episode, I guarantee it. And, we're told again and again that the tanks only have worth insofar as they're useful. 'A very useful' engine, as if being 'useful' to their employers and masters is the only thing they can ever aspire to. And – all this is served up dripping in a kind of cloying Brexity aesthetic on this weird little island, which is actually just some big nostalgic cry-wank for a lost idea of Britain.

Iain Bloody hell.

Zara Thomas the Tank Engine is basically fascism. You've been feeding your kids fascism, mate.

Iain Are any other children's stories fascism?

Zara The Lion King. The Lion King is fascism.

Iain Piss off.

Zara   Fucking is. Circle of Life? That's quasi-religious
propaganda upholding the state's monopoly of violence,
that's what that is. Mufasa is an old-fashioned tyrant.

Iain   So, what's Scar?

Zara   Scar is a vanguardist revolutionary leader aiming to
overthrow the existing hereditary monarchy and feed the
hungry and the marginalised. That's the hyenas. Also, Willy
Wonka? He's a paedo, definitely. I don't have as much textual
evidence for that, but sometimes you just know, don't you.

Iain   How do you know so much about children's stories?

Zara   Niece.

Iain   Right. Well, I have to say, I think it's very much a
shame you didn't go to university. What with your obvious
gift for elaborate contrarian-sounding bollocks. I think you
would have excelled.

Zara   English Literature. Here in Edinburgh. Got a first,
actually, so fuck you.

Iain   Oh. Well. Congratulations.

Zara   Congratulations to you, Iain, it was your idea.

Iain   Sorry?

Zara   I thought your classes were just so fucking inspiring,
you know that?

Iain   Really?

Zara   Don't 'really' me, you knew that.

Iain   I do remember you had a – a special connection. To
the subject.

Zara   I ate up those books you set. *The Catcher in the Rye*.
Fuck me. Very much the choice of a man on a collision
course with a mid-life crisis you could argue, but still. It blew
my mind to be honest.

Iain   You wrote your essay on it. It was really, genuinely
terrific.

Zara He gets a bad rap now the boy in that book, but he's just a broken little kid, isn't he? A broken kid trying to make sense of a fucked up world.

Iain He very much is.

Zara He sees how broken the world is, so full of phonies and bullshit. And he wants to save everyone from it. To catch them, before they fall off the edge.

Iain 'I'd just be the catcher in the rye and all. I know it's crazy.'

Iain *and* **Zara** 'But that's the only thing I'd really like to be.'

Iain When I first read that line as a young man I thought Jesus fucking Christ. That's me. That boy is me.

Zara You tried to catch me I think. Or at least you probably thought that's what you were doing.

Iain What do you mean?

Zara Do you remember what you wrote on my leavers' shirt?

Iain Your –

Zara My shirt. On the last day of school

Iain I . . . I, think –

Zara You don't remember.

Iain I, no. No, sorry.

Zara Course you fucking don't. Well I do. You wrote 'you can do anything you want to do.' That was your message to me. 'To Zara. Dream big. You can do anything you want to do.' It wouldn't even have occurred to me that that might be true, until you told me so. I don't think I'd have even thought to apply to university if you hadn't told me that. You told me I could do anything I want with my life, and I believed you. You did that, Mr Urquhart.

Iain   Well, I – it's a privilege to know that. I'm honoured.

Zara   It was bullshit though, wasn't it.

Iain   I'm sorry?

Zara   Total bullshit. 'You can do anything you want to do.' Written in permanent ink on a girl's school uniform.

Iain   I was trying to encourage you.

Zara   It's a strange way to encourage someone. By furnishing their clothing with lies.

Beat.

Iain   Did any other teachers sign your shirt?

Zara   No. You were the only one that I admired.

Beat.

Iain   Well, if I – if I wrote that, it's because I meant it. Okay? I wanted to help you – to be able to look at the world and see yourself in it, because I thought you were brilliant, and that you deserved that, and nobody else was doing it. And because that is my job as a teacher. To see the best version of a young person, and to prepare them to take that into the world –

Zara   You prepared me for a world that doesn't exist. A fiction. And deep down if you really asked yourself, you probably knew it was all shite. But that was fine. Because it was never about me. It was about you, being the catcher in the fucking rye. Feeling good about yourself. Giving yourself a big pat on the back telling yourself you're not just some deadbeat teacher in a shitey school in Edinburgh, you're fucking Robin Williams in *Dead Poet's Society*. O Captain! My Captain!

Iain   That is all grotesquely unfair.

Zara   You know the most important lesson you learn when you get an Arts and Humanities degree in a collapsing global

economy? That people don't need beauty and art and truth.
What they need is the tools to survive.

Iain   Well pardon me for not being able to predict every
future fluctuation in the economy, but nobody is actually
forcing you to –

Zara   Have you any idea how that feels? That crushing
disappointment in the world?

Iain   I'd say I have more of an idea of that than you could
possibly imagine.

Zara   More bullshit.

Iain   You could get a different job.

Zara   There aren't any jobs, Iain, you dense cunt.

Iain   I've got a job. They're crying out for teachers. You
could –

Zara   Do you like your job? Plugging away at a sub-average
little school in a shit bit of town?

Iain   It's an important job. Doing important work –

Zara   And you are an important man, I get it. Are you still
teaching there?

Iain   Yes. Yes I am, and proud of my long work in that
community –

Zara   Bloody hell. And they've not even promoted you?

Iain   I'm head of department now actually.

Zara   Wow, thirty-odd years and they made you head of
department? You must feel really empowered in your work
situation, must really wake up every day feeling great about
yourself. Haven't *you* ever thought about doing something
else?

Iain   Oh, come on, it's not the same, is it?

Zara   Why not?

Iain   You can't be serious.

Zara   Deadly. Why not?

Iain   Teaching – teaching is a calling. I'm a teacher. I'm a bloody teacher and you're a . . .

Zara   Go on. Say it.

Iain   You're a prostitute, Zara.

Zara   What I do is at least honest –

Iain   Honest, like telling your dad about it honest?

Zara   What are you saying?

Iain   Perhaps he could help?

Zara   What, like he's rich?

Iain   Well, no, but –

Zara   Thank you, Iain but I don't need rescuing, okay, by you, by my dad, or by anyone –

Iain   You could live with him. If you stopped doing this.

Zara   Sure. But I'm a thirty-two year old woman you fucking weird cunt.

Iain   Doesn't it exhaust you, this double life?

Zara   Everyone is exhausted. All work is exhausting.

Iain   Yes but if we're talking about honesty, then for God's sake, Zara, you have to tell your bloody –

Zara   Right.

From a chest of drawers, **Zara** *defiantly pulls out a large brightly-coloured dildo. She places it, erect, on a table near* **Iain**. *Its presence scandalises and terrifies* **Iain**.

Iain   What, what is that, please?

Zara *ignores* **Iain**'s *question and continues pulling out more differently shaped and coloured but equally visually arresting sex toys and placing them on the table as she talks.*

Zara   Both of us sell labour for a wage, okay, something you and I are both unfortunately compelled to do to get by –

She regards each of these objects with an everyday matter-of-factness, like a shop assistant stacking shelves or arranging a window display.

Zara   I work autonomously, independently, and democratically, to look after myself and look after those who work alongside me because that is all there is –

Iain   It's not just work, all this though is it, it's – it's all sex things!

Zara   Uh huh.

Iain   And all the misogyny, and hatred. Hatred of women –

Zara *continues arranging various sex toys and accessories. Butt plugs, prostate massagers, handcuffs . . .*

Zara   I mean, respectfully, you – found the ad on Adult Work dot com I imagine? Or a listings site? Reading the reviews were you?

Iain   I wasn't looking for that though, I was looking for –

Zara   Boys.

Iain   Men. Yes.

Zara   And that's different how?

. . . whips, dildoes made of silicon, rubber, glass, some sculpted and life-like, some abstract and, to **Iain**, *utterly alien-looking.*

Iain   Can you stop this, please? I don't – I don't want any of this sort of thing.

Zara *turns to face* **Iain** *and casually picks up her phone and takes a photograph of him.*

Iain   What, what, what are you doing? What is that?

Zara   That is a photograph of a respectable local high school teacher surrounded by a smorgasbord of glistening dildoes and esoteric fetish gear, that's what that is.

Iain   You –

Zara   I normally wouldn't –

Iain   What!

Zara   I normally wouldn't –

Iain   Oh God.

Zara   I normally wouldn't do this sort of thing but you've been quite, quite disrespectful towards me, Iain, and now you're making a lot of noises about telling my dad, and I absolutely cannot allow that to happen, so –

Iain   Give that to me. Give it to me.

Zara   No. It's an insurance policy.

Iain   Delete that. Zara. Delete that at once.

Zara   I can't do that, sorry.

Iain   You little –

Zara   What? Little what?

Iain   You wouldn't dare. Stop playing games. You're full of shit.

Zara   Am I?

Iain   You don't want that photo getting out any more than I do. Do you? Because it'll get back to you. You use that against me and what's stopping me telling the whole world about you? About what you've become.

Zara   Well at least I've not become a big stupid lying phony arsehole.

Iain   Listen to yourself. You have been so keen to tell me how all of this is my fault. How the world has let you down, how your teachers have let you down, how society has let *you* down. Come on. Take some responsibility for yourself, Zara!

Zara   Easy for you to say! The world has changed, Iain. Your generation had comparatively, some kind of fucking security – we don't. Just stuck forever in a dystopian gig economy nightmare. We're always told we're failing, at being adults. We're not 'bad at adulting' we've just become adults in a world that's falling to shit. Do you even hear yourself? Talking about teaching young people to imagine bright futures like the future isn't overwhelmingly, catastrophically fucked. Did you ever think of that? That's the difference, for us. You never had to contend with the existential reality of an actual impending apocalypse. It's kind of a game-changer –

Iain   You never heard of the Cold War? The nuclear threat?

Off, a sound of a baby crying.

Iain   Everyone always grows up thinking it's the end of the world. The only difference with you lot is you think it makes you special –

The door is barged open.

*In charges **Jay**. Wiry and wired. He is carrying a baby in a Moses basket. The kid is wailing the fucking roof down. **Jay** has the furious, exasperated, desperate, manic, and utterly defeated energy of a man who has long since given up on trying to get the child to go back to sleep.*

Zara   What the fuck do you call this?

Jay   Shut up.

*The baby cries. **Jay** places the Moses basket down and rubs his temples. He opens a half-drunk bottle of Coke and necks some.*

Zara   Seriously, what the fuck are you –

Jay   Shut up I said!

The baby cries.

Right.

Like a badly bruised boxer stepping back into the ring, **Jay** *tries again. He lifts the baby out of the Moses basket and starts pacing up and down the room.*

Jay   Sh, sh, sh. Come on now, sh, sh, sh –

Zara   Jay, what is going on?

Jay   Will everyone fucking shut up, I said! Christ!

The baby cries. **Jay** *paces and shushes.*

Iain   Is this . . . is this him?

Zara   The boy you ordered. I'm sorry.

Iain   Right.

Jay   I was promised she would fall asleep on the way over. They promised. Said, she hasn't had a nap, she'll go straight to sleep, she'll be asleep for two hours. Lies!

Zara   You're not meant to fucking bring her here in the first place, you know that.

Jay   I didn't have a choice! She was meant to be asleep! Will you please shut up! I've checked her nappy. Nothing. Changed it anyway. Tried the bottle. Not interested.

He holds the baby up to his face, desperate.

Jay   What do you want? What is it you actually want?!

Iain   Could be colic.

Jay   Did I fucking ask you?!

Iain   Just trying to help.

Jay   Who is this? Is he a doctor? Is he the fucking baby doctor? Eh?

Zara This is the guy.

Jay Well tell him to shut his hole! Can we put that in the ground rules? No running over time, nothing without protection, and no fucking unsolicited parenting advice! Thank you!

The baby cries.

Zara Iain, can you give us a minute?

Iain This is ridiculous. I'm sorry, but however crudely I am in fact paying for a service of some, of some description here, and I don't think, I don't think I should be spoken to like –

Zara You're quite right. You're quite right of course. We'll discuss a discount –

Jay No, we will not discuss a fucking discount!

The baby cries. **Zara** *shepherds* **Iain** *towards the bathroom door.*

Zara We will discuss a discount, but please give me a moment. With apologies, if you could step this way please Mr Urquhart.

Iain Ridiculous.

Zara You can get ready in here, there's a shower if you want it, everything you need. Okay?

Zara *closes the door on* **Iain** *and locks it from the outside.*

Zara Right, so here what the fuck!

Jay Don't start, please! And also fuck you.

Zara Excuse me?

Jay You've still not paid me for last time.

Zara Take your fucking shoes off.

Jay What?

Zara Shoes off, you cunt!

Jay *kicks his shoes off.*

Zara   Why the fuck have you brought your fucking sprog to fucking work, Jay? What the fuck are you doing?

Jay   Didn't have a choice.

Zara   Did you get my message? I've been sat here, with a completely new client –

Jay   I came as fast as I could –

The baby cries.

Zara   – working my arse off to stop him from getting up and walking out the door, when it would have been much easier for me to let him go instead of putting up with his bullshit –

Jay   Right, okay –

Zara   I would never, ever put you in that situation and you know it. We have rules, Jay. For safety. That's why we work together. And now you come charging in with your fucking dickhead kid shitting all over everything –

Jay   Hey! Watch it!

Zara   Like, what are you thinking! You fucking idiot!

Jay   I didn't have a choice! Her mum has a trial shift, I said I'd take her, she's already threatening to cut me out. What was I supposed to do?

Zara   Why didn't you say? Give me a heads up or something? Did you even get my message –

Jay   Phone battery died, on the bus. Do you have a charger? Android.

Zara   No. iPhone.

Jay   Oh fuck off, man! And anyway, you can keep your workers' co-op mutual rules shit. You owe me my pay!

Zara   What? You said I could settle you up after a couple of days just this once, for cashflow, we agreed this –

Jay   No. I want it up front every day now, or nothing. I've changed my mind.

Zara   You can't just do that –

Jay   Why not? It's my money.

Zara   Listen. The rent is going up, okay? Like way up.

Jay   And? What's my pay got to do with your fucking rent?

Zara   We both take a bit off the top to cover overheads, Jay, including using this place. And I do a lot of fucking work on the admin side you know, not to mention the bills, and the risk factor. And the rent just fucking doubled, so –

Jay   So fucking, move then!

Zara   Even if I move, it'll be more expensive! Do you read the fucking news?

Jay   What? No!

Zara   Look, I've been trying to help you, Jay. You've a brand new client in there. He could've left, but I kept him here. Because you need him. You've not been bringing in enough, simple as that, I'm sorry.

Jay   Oh, I see how it is. Fucking collectivized equal rights, horse shit! You're just like any other prick. Just like any other fucking boss. I see you. You're fucking me, and you've always been fucking me!

Zara   What?

Jay   Taking a cut. Telling me when I can get paid, skimming a bit off for yourself –

Zara   I've got overheads!

Jay   Sure, sure.

Zara   We're a co-op working under a mutually agreed set of principles, and if we're gonna review those principles, then –

Jay   I'm not interested. 'Mutually agreed set of principles. Equal share. Safer spaces policy.' You're full of shit. I know the score. My name is Jay and my pronouns are pay/me!

The baby cries.

Jay   Please! Stop!

Zara   Have you tried winding her?

Jay   Yes! Fuck off!

Zara   You're getting older, Jay, and you're struggling. I'm sorry but –

Jay   Fuck you!

Zara   Your clients want a young, pretty, little twink –

Jay   And? That's what I give them.

Zara   It was fine when you were younger. But there's a shelf-life on boys like you, that's just how it is, sorry. You need to think about some kind of . . . vibe shift.

Jay   And what, I just bulk up, grow a beard, become some kind of bear is that it? Some kind of daddy? And are you paying for that steroid subscription, I take it? Is that coming out of our shared overheads?

The baby cries.

Zara   Look, give her here.

Zara *takes the baby. The baby continues to cry.*

I've been trying to help you but I'm not a fucking charity. Shush, shush, it's okay –

Jay   I need my money. For her. She said if I don't start paying my way, she'll cut me off, completely. Do you understand what that means? Time to man up she said. So that's what's happening. From now on. How's that for a vibe shift? When I leave here, I'm bringing her back to her mum and I'm handing her over with a wad of cash that I earned. Do you get that? Or else maybe I will fuck off. Do my own thing.

Zara   Right. How you gonna manage that then?

Jay   Dunno. OnlyFans.

Zara   You don't make shit on OnlyFans.

Jay   Well neither do you!

Zara   I can't make shit on OnlyFans, because anonymous accounts aren't worth shit –

Jay   Stop being such a fucking little bitch and get your face on there then.

Zara   I've got to stay anonymous or my dad will –

The baby cries.

Jay   She doesn't like being held like that, here, here –

Jay *takes the baby back. She continues to cry.*

Zara   Anyway you've got your face and name on OnlyFans and you still can't make shit.

Jay   Nobody can make shit on OnlyFans cos it's a fucking Ponzi scheme!

Zara   Which is why you need this place and you need *me* –

Iain *bangs on the door.*

Iain (*off*)   Excuse me! Excuse me but what is going on?

Zara   Right. Fucking listen. The guy you've got there, some things you need to know about him. He's nervous. Confused. Obviously a bit lost, you know the type.

Jay   Oh Christ.

Zara   But listen, if he has a good time, I think he would probably come back. Like, maybe a lot I reckon. If you can figure out what he wants. He's in that exact sweet spot of personal crisis where he's looking for something, you know, and if he thinks you're giving him it –

Jay   He could be regular.

Zara   He could be very fucking regular.

Beat.

Jay   Right. Okay. Right.

Zara   He's a total newbie though so it could go either way. He has tried to leave already.

Jay   Right.

Zara   And I did soak him with a strawberry yoghurt drink.

Jay   What? Why?

Zara   Accident. Also, he's my old schoolteacher.

Jay   Fuck off. Another one?

The baby cries louder.

Argh! Please, please, stop!

Zara   Do you want me to take her again?

Jay   No! I know what I'm doing! Why does everybody think I don't know what I'm doing!

Iain *tries to open the door. It doesn't open. He knocks.*

Iain (*off*)   I've had quite enough of this now if you don't mind!

Zara   Come here look, look –

She takes the baby.

Sshhh, shhhh, there we go, shhhh. I know. Daddy's just stressed. It's okay. It's okay.

The crying calms.

See? There we go. It's okay. Daddy has to go to work now.
It's okay. Shhhh. Shhhh. I'm sorry I called you his dickhead
kid, you're lovely really. It's not your fault daddy is an
absolute rocket. You're lovely. Yes you are. Shhhh. Shhhh.

The crying stops. She continues to rock the baby in her arms.

There we go. There we go.

Silence.

Jay I hate you for that you know.

Pause.

But thank you.

Zara She just wanted a change of energy. You were
panicking, that's all.

Jay I know what I'm doing.

Zara I know you do.

Jay I'm a good dad.

Zara I know. I know.

Pause.

That's her.

*She delicately passes the baby to **Jay**, who carefully and lovingly lays
her down in the Moses basket. She is asleep. They both look at her.*

Jay I just love her so much, you know?

Iain *bangs on the door, increasingly distressed.*

Iain (*off*) Let me out of here! Let me out!

Zara Listen, he's very rattled. I'll lend you my phone, if he
pulls funny shit.

Zara *hands her phone to **Jay**. The photo of **Iain** is still up onscreen.*

Jay Yikes. Nice photo.

Iain (*off*)   This is fast becoming a hostage situation! Let me out!

Zara *gestures to the door to the hall.*

Zara   Get out there a minute.

Jay *heads into the hall, taking the phone with him. He closes the door.* **Iain** *bangs.* **Zara** *opens the door to the bathroom.* **Iain** *spills out.*

Zara   We were just trying to get the baby to sleep Mr Urquhart, apologies for the inconvenience. Everything is fine.

Iain   Why is there a baby here?

Zara   This is a residential property, people live here. Sometimes there's a baby here.

Iain   I –

Zara   Sit down a minute. Jay will be with you momentarily.

Iain *sits.* **Zara** *heads out to the hall, where* **Jay** *is.*

Iain   Bloody hell.

Silence. **Iain** *considers his surroundings. He considers the table full of multiple glistening dildoes. He tentatively selects one; a great big gleaming wobbly purple number. He picks it up. It undulates obscenely in his quivering hand. He is transfixed. Slowly, cautiously, he pulls his face towards it and gingerly sniffs the oscillating tip. But then!* **Zara** *and* **Jay** *re-enter –*

Zara   Okay, Iain –

Iain *squeals! He drops the dildo and stands in shock – knocking the entire pristine arrangement to the floor as he does: an almighty cascade of bouncing plastic cocks crashing around his feet.*

Silence.

Jay   Wow.

Beat.

Iain   I suppose I'd better pick those up.

Zara   Yes, I suppose so.

Iain   Okay. Okay then.

Iain *painfully, shamefully, sets about picking up each of the fallen members, one by one, and re-arranging them carefully on the table, his hands shaking clumsily as he does. He continues in this excruciating task as* **Zara** *speaks.*

Zara   Okay, Iain. You've got forty-five minutes with Jay. Some ground rules. Jay only bottoms, you should know that from the ad. Please only use the rubbers we provide, they're extra thick and safer for anal sex – sorry if that's obvious, but lots of men do come here having only ever had extremely missionary hetero sex before, and so some things do need to be pointed out. If you're not familiar with anything or need help then Jay will be very happy to assist you. We will stop with all this kind of contractual chat once I start the clock, I know it's a buzzkill but believe me it's better to get it clear now than to have to break midway through to discuss the small print. There's an extra fee on certain things, if you ask Jay to suck you off he will, but it will cost extra. However, if it pleases you, he can wank you off just now to start for no extra charge. Any questions?

Beat.

Jay, I'm just on the other side of the door. If I don't hear from you five minutes after time I'll knock and check in on you, okay? I'll leave you both to it.

Zara *picks up the baby carrier, and leaves. Pause.*

Iain   Hello.

Jay   Sorry I'm late.

Iain   Yes. Yes. You really were quite late.

Jay   Sorry.

Iain   Okay.

Beat.

That your kid then?

Jay   Forget about that, don't worry. It's fine.

Iain   Right. It's just . . .

Jay   What?

Iain   It's just it sort of . . . I don't know. Ruins something a bit, doesn't it.

Jay   Forget about it. Honestly. It's fine.

Iain   Quite a lot of . . . reality. Encroaching on the experience.

Jay   Just let it go. She's gone. She's not here. Just you and me, Iain.

Iain   I said to her 'a boy' I said. Wanted a boy, you see.

Jay   And here he is. Ta-daa.

Iain   Sort of weird that you're someone's dad.

Jay   Look, fucking –

Iain   Sorry. It just is. What age are you?

Jay   Young.

Beat.

I'm a young, young boy.

Beat.

I'm twenty-two.

Beat.

Okay fine, I'm twenty-six.

Beat.

I'm thirty.

Iain   Right.

Beat.

What do we do now?

Jay   Well. You're supposed to tell me, mister. This your first time, is it?

Iain   Yes.

Jay   Right well.

Jay, *taking control of the situation, shifts into more deliberate performance mode.*

Shall I wank you off, Iain?

Iain *shakes his head.*

Jay   What would you like to do? What would you like me to do to you?

Iain *stands. Nervous. Uncertain.*

Jay   What would you like to do to me? It's okay. You tell me.

Beat.

What will I call you? Do you want me to call you anything?

Iain   No.

Beat.

Iain's fine.

Jay   Okay, Iain.

Jay *steps close to* **Iain**. **Iain** *trembles.*

Jay   Would you like to sit with me on the bed, Iain?

Beat. **Iain** *sits.* **Jay** *joins him.*

Jay   What will I do now, Iain? What do you want me to do?

Iain *sighs a shuddering sigh.*

Iain   Um, I. Dunno.

Jay   It's okay.

Iain   Sorry.

Jay   It's okay.

Iain   I'm sorry. It's – in the videos, it's all – I watch videos. And the young men look so . . . happy I suppose. Free.

Jay   And you wanted to feel something like that. You watch the videos and you feel . . . what? Jealous?

Iain   I suppose lots of people do.

Jay *tenderly takes* **Iain***'s hand. Lovingly, understandingly.*

Jay   I can help you find out what you want, Iain.

Beat.

We can feel free, together, Iain. You and me.

Iain *sighs, trembling.*

Jay   Why don't you start by taking your shirt off?

Iain   S'pose.

Iain *starts unbuttoning his shirt. His hand quivers.*

Jay   I can do it. If you would like that?

Beat.

Iain   Okay.

Jay *starts unbuttoning* **Iain***'s shirt.* **Iain** *sits tense and rigid.* **Jay** *puts his hand on* **Iain***'s thigh. He strokes his thigh, coquettishly.* **Iain** *smiles nervously.* **Jay** *moves closer.*

Jay   Do you like that, Iain?

Iain   I . . .

Jay   Can I kiss you? I'd love to kiss you.

Beat. **Jay** *kisses* **Iain.** **Iain** *freezes up, awkwardly, lips pursed.* **Jay** *keeps trying. He kisses his neck. He caresses his inner thigh. He tries again, kissing* **Iain***'s tense frozen lips as luxuriously as he can manage.* **Jay** *gives up. Frustrated and dejected. He puts the game face back on, tries again.*

Jay   I want to give you what you want, Iain.

Pause. **Iain** *says nothing.* **Jay** *gestures to the table of dildoes.*

Jay   You looked interested in my little buddies here earlier.

Iain   No. I don't want that stuff. I'm not a pervert!

Jay   Okay. Okay. It's just toys, it's –

Iain   I'm just an extremely normal man.

Jay   Yes. Right.

Iain   I'm a very normal man and you all keep making out like I'm something else. Something not that. Some kind of sex freak. With your rules and your toys and your kink stuff. It's not who I am. It's not.

Iain *turns away from* **Jay.** **Jay** *considers. He tries something.*

Jay   Are you sure about that, Iain?

Beat.

Jay   Who are you, Iain?

Beat.

Iain   I don't know.

Jay   Are you a pervert, Iain?

Beat.

Iain   I don't know.

Jay   A filth merchant? A freak? A disgusting little fuck?

Beat.

Iain   Maybe. Maybe I am.

Jay   Yes. You are, aren't you Iain? You're a fucking dirty little cunt. That's who you are.

Iain   I honestly don't know.

Jay   Oh we can have fun, Iain. I can make you feel whatever you want in here, you sick nasty little puppy. You're a nasty little puppy, aren't you, Iain?

Jay *approaches* **Iain***, he pushes him onto the bed. He straddles him.*

Jay   This is it isn't it? This is what you want.

He bites his chest.

Iain   Ow!

Jay   You want it like this, you horrible little turnip –

Iain   No! I don't.

Jay   What?

Iain   I don't want this.

Jay *drops out of performance mode suddenly, exasperated.*

Jay   Oh for fuck's sake . . .

Iain   I'm sorry.

Jay   Right. Okay. Look, fucking, I dunno then.

Pause.

Iain   Horrible little turnip?

Jay   I was trying something.

Iain   Sure.

Jay   So what now?

Pause.

Iain   Can we try just, talking first?

Jay   Talking?

Iain   Yes. And see where it goes.

Jay   Na, na, na. Listen, I'm sorry but I know what you're like, men like you. Zara warned me you might get like this.

Iain   Like what?

Jay   You wanna chat, you wanna take things slowly, you wanna play getting to know you and then, bang! Time's up, and you start kicking off that you didn't get your money's worth. Start talking shit and demanding refunds. Well, no. We're not having that. So take off your trousers for a start.

Iain   Excuse me?

Jay   I said take off your trousers, I'm not having this.

Iain   But she said . . . Zara. Zara said sometimes. Other men. They just. They just talk.

Jay   No. Zara talks. I don't. She told me to get her if I started feeling weird. And I'm feeling pretty weird. I don't understand you. I don't know what you want.

Iain   I'm just talking.

Jay   She said if you started any funny business I was to –

Iain   Fine.

Jay   No funny business.

Beat.

Iain   If I . . . if I take off my clothes. Can we talk?

Beat.

Jay   You're not going to ask for a refund?

Iain   No.

Jay   Promise?

Iain   Promise.

Jay   I'm not very good at talking.

Iain   Right.

Jay   It's not really what I do.

Iain   That's okay.

Jay   Right. Fine.

Iain   Okay.

Jay   Okay.

Iain   Okay then.

Jay   Take off your shirt.

Pause. **Iain** *removes his shirt.*

Jay   And the trousers.

Iain *removes his trousers.*

Jay   And the rest.

Iain *removes his underpants. He stands in only his socks.*

Jay   Right.

Iain   Right.

Beat.

Are you going to take your clothes off, or . . .?

Jay   Do you want me to?

Iain *shrugs.*

Iain   Seems fair?

Jay   Great.

Jay *takes off his shirt. His socks. His trousers. His underpants. They both stand naked, a distance apart.*

So, Iain. What is it you want to talk about?

Iain   Anything really. You? Talk about you? Tell me something about you.

Jay   I don't have anything to say about me. What else?

Beat. **Jay** *tries to do what he thinks* **Iain** *wants.*

Jay   Do you like . . . fucking, I dunno. Politics?

Iain   Not much. You come to realise they're all the same really, after a while.

Jay   Yeah, I agree.

Iain   Sorry?

Jay   I said I agree.

Iain   Right. Great.

Pause.

Jay   What about films?

Iain   Films?

Jay   Yeah. What's your favourite film? Let me guess. Godfather.

Iain   Top Gun.

Jay   Ah.

Beat.

Jay   Football? Who do you support?

Iain   Hearts.

Jay   Right.

Pause.

Jay   This is weird.

Iain   It's really weird, isn't it?

Jay   It was your idea.

Iain   Not the naked bit.

Jay   Well, you did come to a brothel to do this, in fairness.

Iain   Yes.

Jay   And it was you that wanted to talk.

Iain   Right.

Jay   So what else?

Pause.

Jay   Maybe, tell me about your kids?

Iain   My kids?

Jay   Yeah. You have kids?

Iain   Two.

Jay   Boys or girls?

Iain   Daughters, both. Not girls anymore, they're grown up.

Beat.

Jay   What's it like, when they grow up?

Iain   Heart-breaking.

Jay   Right.

Iain   They say it takes a village to raise a child. But there isn't a village. There's just you parents. And you're both so tired all the time having to work to do everything. Everything.

Jay   I suppose.

Iain   And you pour everything into setting things up for them the way you think their life is supposed to look, trying never to complain about it. Preparing them, protecting them from the world. But of course they wind up just the same as all the other little shits you see at school because of course they do. Slipping further and further into a world you don't understand and then one day they're gone. And that's it.

And it's just the two of you again. And all that's left is the resentment.

Jay   I see.

Beat.

Do they call you, sometimes?

Iain   Who?

Jay   Your daughters.

Iain   No. Not really.

Jay   Right.

Iain *starts dressing again. He puts his underpants back on.*

Jay   Nobody really prepares you for anything with this, do they?

Iain   What do you mean?

Jay   Nothing. Your wife, she –

Iain   Hates me.

Jay   Actual?

Iain   I think so, yes. Underneath it all. Never used to I don't think, but so it goes. She told me, she said to me, why don't you quit your bloody job then if it's making you so depressed. We can retire early, move to the seaside. But it's what I have. My job. It's who I am, and it's what I have.

Jay   Or maybe you just don't want to be stuck at the seaside alone with someone who hates you, both of you waiting to die.

Pause. **Jay** *starts dressing again.* **Iain** *considers* **Jay**.

Iain   You're very beautiful.

Jay   Thank you. So are you, Iain.

Iain   You're just saying that because I'm paying you.

Jay   It sort of ruins it if you say that.

Iain   Right.

Beat. **Jay** *tries something.*

Jay   Look at me again, Iain.

Iain *looks at* **Jay**.

Jay   Am I beautiful?

Iain *nods.*

Iain   Yes.

Jay   Would you like me to come closer?

Iain   Yes.

Jay *walks closer to* **Iain**.

Jay   What's beautiful about me?

Iain   You have beautiful eyes.

Jay   Thank you.

Iain   I used to think, with my wife. That sex was just. It was so, pointless that really, all it was for was just a chance to look into someone else's eyes. For a bit.

Jay   That's lovely.

Iain   Is it?

Jay   I think so.

Iain   I think it's tragic.

They stare into each other's eyes.

Jay   Is this tragic?

Iain   No. No.

Iain *reaches out and touches* **Jay**'s *face. He sighs.*

You . . .

Jay   Yes?

Iain   You . . . you were late you know.

Jay   Was I?

Iain   Uh huh.

Jay   Did that disappoint you?

Iain   Yes.

Jay   Like how you're disappointed in your kids?

Iain   . . . Yes.

Jay   And your students?

Iain   Yes.

Jay   You're angry aren't you, Iain? There's a lot of anger in you.

Iain   There's a lot of anger in everyone.

Jay   Those happy, happy boys in the videos. Are they angry?

Iain   I don't know.

Jay   Are you angry at them?

Iain   Yes.

Jay   Are you angry at them for being happy? And free?

Iain   Yes.

Jay   The bastards.

Iain   The little fucking bastards.

Jay   The ungrateful little shits.

Iain   Yes.

Jay   How dare they? How dare they be so carefree and abandoned and disgusting?

Iain   Yes.

Jay   When you have to feel so trapped? When you've had to work so hard? You'd like to wipe the smile off their faces.

Iain   Yes.

Jay   Are you angry at me, Iain?

Iain   Yes.

Jay   For being late?

Iain   You were late.

Jay   For having the cheek, the insolence!

Iain   I was waiting. You shouldn't have left me waiting.

Jay   Did I disappoint you?

Iain   You did.

Jay   Was it very bad of me?

Iain   It was!

Jay   Am I very bad? Daddy?

Iain   You are!

Jay   You like it when I call you that don't you, really? Daddy?

Iain   Yes!

Jay   Okay then. Daddy. Was I very, very bad?

Iain   Yes!

Jay   Am I a bad irresponsible child?

Iain   Yes. Yes you are!

Jay   Tell me what I am!

Iain   You're a bad, irresponsible . . . young man!

Jay   I think I deserve to be punished. Is that what you want? You want to punish me? Punish my beautiful face?

Iain Yes.

Jay Like in the videos?

Iain Yes!

Jay Destroy me?

Iain Yes!

Jay Because I deserve it?

Iain You deserve it. You all fucking deserve it!

Jay Tell me what I deserve, Daddy. Sir.

Iain You deserve to be punished! All of you. But especially you.

Jay Because I disappoint you?

Iain Because you disgust me!

Jay Do I? Please don't punish me. I'll do anything you want, Daddy. Do you want me to get my knees, do I need to beg you?

Iain On your knees! Get on your knees and say you're sorry!

Jay Oh yes, Daddy!

Jay *gets on to his knees.*

Jay I'm sorry! I'm so sorry, Daddy! I've been so naughty!

Iain Beg for forgiveness!

Jay Please forgive me, Sir. I'll do anything!

Iain You're a despicable ungrateful piece of shit! What are you?

Jay I'm a despicable ungrateful piece of shit, Sir!

The baby cries.

Tell me how you're going to punish me!

The baby cries.

I want to get what's coming to me. I want you to destroy me!

The baby cries.

Iain   The . . . your baby.

Jay   Give me what's coming to me. Teach me a lesson, Daddy.

The baby cries.

Iain   Uh . . .

Jay   Don't worry about that. Stay here. Stay with this. It's just me and you in here, and I've been very, very bad, Sir!

The baby cries.

Do you hate me?

The baby cries.

Do I disgust you?

Iain   Oh come on, doesn't it make you feel some kind of fucking shame?

Jay   What?

Iain   Bringing her, to a place like this? I mean look at you. Look at yourself, you stupid little twerp!

Jay   Am I a twerp? Am I a cretin? Am I revolting to you, Daddy?

Iain   Yes! You fucking are! That's your child crying out there and you're scrambling about like this? Like a fucking insect! On your knees? For money! What is wrong with you?

Jay   Is this still part of it, or . . .?

Iain   Bringing a child, your baby. To this! This debauched house of filth. That, that baby deserves better. Than you. Than any of this. Listen to that. Listen.

The baby cries.

How does that make you feel?

Jay   I'm doing my best.

Iain   Yes, well, that's all any of us are doing, isn't it? You never think about how you ended up here? Like this? The way you are? Humiliating yourself like this? And her in there. Left with nothing but you to rely on. Look at you. You pathetic, abject failure of a man. You disgrace of a father. If they took her away from you it would be a blessing.

The baby cries. **Jay** *sits on all fours, humiliated, seething. Repressing a red mist that rises in him.*

Jay   Okay then.

Iain*'s phone starts ringing.*

Iain   My wife. It'll be my wife.

Jay   Well, you better answer it then. Sir.

Iain *reaches into the pocket of his crumpled trousers and answers the phone.* **Jay** *watches* **Iain**, *festering in anger.*

Iain   Hello? Hello, darling. Yes indeed. No, no, nothing wrong. What? I'm not being strange. I went for a drink. An after-work drink. I'm really sorry, I thought I'd texted you. What meeting? The financial planner, yes. Oh, I'm sorry. I'm so sorry I . . . No.

Jay *decides.*

Jay (*to himself*)   Fuck it.

He gets up.

Iain   No, I'm just. I'm on the street, going to, uh. Catch a bus.

Jay *picks up* **Zara***'s phone.*

Iain   Well, I don't know. I don't know why you can't hear anything.

Iain, *on the phone, doesn't notice as* **Jay** *swipes, punches a few keys.*

Jay (*to himself*)   Who's the disgrace now, dickhead.

Jay *tosses the phone back on to the heap of clothes.* **Jay** *turns to look at* **Iain**, *satisfied.*

Iain   Listen, I've got to go. I've got to catch this, uh, catch this bus. Yes. I'm getting on it now, okay? Okay. Love you. Bye. Byeee.

He hangs up. Beat.

Shit.

He tosses his phone on to the sofa.

I forgot about our meeting.

Jay   With the financial planner.

Iain   Yes. It's about consolidating our pensions.

Jay   Uh huh.

Beat.

So, are you going, or?

Iain   We had an argument. Last night. Big fight really. It started because I spoke about getting divorced.

Jay   Yeah that'll do it.

Iain   I didn't mean it really. It wasn't like . . . I'd had a drink. A sort of wistful, 'Do you ever imagine?' Like, 'Do you ever imagine what it'd be like? If we'd never met. If we had been given, sort of given, a different life?' Maybe it didn't come out like that. I don't know. 'How would it have been?' Sort of thing.

Beat.

To look at me, I should be happy. Shouldn't I?

Jay   Sure.

Iain   I have done the right things. I work hard. I've done everything right by anyone in my life. I have a wife and two adult children who are – sort of fine, I suppose. A nice enough house. It's what it's supposed to look like isn't it.

Jay   I honestly don't fucking know, Iain.

Iain   So why is it all so . . . shit. Loveless. Lying next to someone who hates you, in the same bed every night. Pretending.

Jay   Well. It can always get worse.

The baby cries.

Iain   This isn't really working for me. I really have made a stupid fucking mistake, coming here.

Iain *gets up. He continues putting his clothes back on.*

This has been a very, very strange afternoon.

Jay   No refunds.

Zara *bursts in, with a tablet in her hand.*

Zara   What the fuck is this?!

Iain *instinctively tries to cover himself up.*

Iain   Nothing! I mean, we were just . . .

Zara   I mean this. You posted it!

Jay   Yeah.

Zara   From my fucking Facebook.

Iain   Posted what?

Jay   He deserved it.

Iain   Deserved what?

Zara   What the fuck were you thinking?

Iain   Deserved what?

Zara   It's a picture of my old high school teacher, standing next to a stack of sex toys in my bedroom –

Iain   I'm sorry, what?

Jay   You can't tell what room it's in, chill out.

Zara   It's from my fucking Facebook!

Jay   Oh, oh right. Shit. Sorry.

Iain   What?

Zara   Look!

She holds the phone out for **Iain** *to see. He looks like he's seen a ghost.*

Iain   Well, delete it then!

Zara   I have, genius! But it's already been copied and shared to your page!

Iain   No. No!

Jay   I suppose you'll have a lot of mutuals –

Zara   Yes! Obviously!

Jay   – cos of school and that.

Iain *scrambles with his phone.* **Zara** *stands in stunned shock.*

Iain   How – how do I stop that? Surely I can stop that.

Jay   Oh fuck.

Iain   Argh!

Iain *hurls himself at* **Jay**, *with alarming strength.*

Zara   Mr Urquhart.

Iain   You devil! You demon! You destroyer of –

They wrestle, **Jay** *struggling to free himself from* **Iain**'s *grip, lashing his limbs around.*

Iain *sticks the head on* **Jay**, *who collapses to the floor.*

Jay   Argh! Fuck!

Iain, *violence flowing through him, lunges at* **Jay**. **Zara** *grabs a massive glass dildo from the dildo table –*

Zara   Fucking old cunt!

Fucko! **Zara** *cunts* **Iain** *across the head with the dildo. He lies on the floor, still.*

Jay   Oh shit! What have you done?

Zara   What?

Jay   To him?

Zara   I don't know! I hit him! With this!

Jay   Is he dead?

Zara   I don't know!

Jay *gets up. They stare at* **Iain**.

Zara   How do you tell?

Jay *cautiously approaches* **Iain**. **Iain** *groans.*

Jay   Not dead. Okay. Not dead, he's not dead.

Zara   Okay, good.

Jay   Not dead is good.

Zara   Is it?

Jay   I don't know. Yes? Isn't it?

Zara   I don't know!

Jay   That is cold, mate. That is fucking cold. You're a stone-cold killer!

Zara   I didn't kill him, you said he's not dead!

Jay   You could've done! And then you said that maybe it was good!

Zara   I don't know! I panicked!

Jay   Well, what do we do now, does he need an ambulance or what?

Zara   If we call an ambulance they'll call the cops!

Jay   That's your problem.

Zara   What!

Jay   You're the one who smacked him! And, and you're the one who'll get done for brothel-keeping. Not my fucking problem is it!

Zara   You're an accessory! And what are you gonna do for money anyway, if you can't work here? Did you think any of this through?

Jay   No! Obviously! He called me a bad dad –

Zara   Jesus Christ. Has he broken anything? Have I cracked his skull?

Jay   He's not bleeding.

Zara   Right. Well. Okay.

Jay   Okay. Should we try to wake him up?

Zara   No!

Jay   Why not?

Zara   What if he goes to the police?

Jay   Oh fuck. We should just run. Leave him here and run.

Zara   Okay. Okay. Where?

Jay   I dunno, like. Home.

Zara   I live here!

Jay   Oh yeah. We could dump him somewhere.

Zara   Where?

Jay   Outside. Like in a bin or something.

Zara   A fucking bin?

Jay   I dunno!

Iain   No, please –

Zara   He's waking up. We have to stop him.

Jay   Okay. Really? Like, stop him?

Zara   Yes, we have to fucking stop him!

Jay   Yeah, but do you mean like 'stop him' stop him?

Zara   I don't know what sort of 'stop him' do you mean?

Jay   That's what I'm asking you!

Zara   Do you think I'm saying we need to 'stop him'?

Jay   Yes! Are you?

Zara   I do think that unless we want him to go to the cops then yes, we need to stop him!

Jay   Because that is heavy fucking duty and I don't know if I have it in me to –

Zara   I'm not saying we should fucking kill him, for fuck sake, Jay!

Jay   Well, what are you fucking saying then!

Zara's *phone rings. They stare at it. They stare at each other.* **Jay** *picks up* **Zara**'s *phone.*

Jay   It's your dad.

Zara   I'm dead. You've killed me. I'm actually dead.

Jay   He . . . might have been ringing about something else?

Zara   That picture will be getting shared about the internet, around the school, Facebook groups of former pupils –

Jay   Okay, I get it.

Zara's *phone keeps ringing.*

Zara   Give it here.

Jay   No.

Zara   Give it here!

Jay   Don't answer it yet. Get your story straight first.

Zara   What are you talking about –

Jay   Just hear me out! You can pin it on me, okay?

Zara   What?

Jay   I'm serious. Why the fuck not?

The phone stops ringing.

Zara   He'll be leaving a message, probably.

Long silence. The phone buzzes.

Jay   That's the voicemail come through

Iain   I . . .

Jay   It's like this: your mate was staying over. He was having an affair with an older man, who, who – would you ever believe, it just turns out was whatshisname from school –

Zara   Mr Urquhart.

Jay   Mr Urquhart. You had no idea, he brought him back. Completely unbeknownst to you! Some co-incidence, eh Dad? A small city this after all! Your mate, he'd brought all his own mental sex toys – it's some sort of gay thing, Dad, you don't need to understand – and then when he used your phone to take a picture, it automatically uh, uploaded uh, to –

Zara   Why would he believe any of that?

Jay   'If you don't believe me, Dad, here's my friend Jay to explain himself! Ex-friend really, lol! I know it sounds ridiculous but it won't happen again' etcetera, etcetera.

Zara   You'd do that?

Jay   Easy.

Zara   Christ. You're going to help me?

Jay   I will. I'll help you with your dad, I'll help you with him.

Zara   Okay. Okay. Thank you. Thank you –

Jay   But not until you give me the money you owe me.

Zara   What?

Jay   Threefold, actually.

Zara   Fucking hell, Jay!

Jay   See it as an advance but I want it all now.

Zara   No way.

Jay   When I drop her off with her mum, I'm handing her over with a bag of cash that I earned.

Zara   You're fucking unbelievable.

Jay   And if you don't like it, I'm heading out this door right now and leaving him, and your old man, to you.

Zara   You fucking cunt!

Jay   Business is business, Zara.

Zara   I hate you sometimes, do you know that.

Jay *starts putting on his shoes.*

Zara   Fuck it. Fuck it then, fine. It's yours.

Jay   Right. I'm taking his phone for a start.

Jay *takes* **Iain***'s phone.*

Iain   . . . What.

Jay *and* **Zara** *look at each other.*

Iain   What is this?

Jay   Hi, Iain.

Iain *looks at* **Jay**, *dazed. Remembers where he is. Touches his head.*

Jay   Iain. Iain, it's okay.

Iain   Get away from me! Ah, Jesus Christ . . .

In a dizzy panic, **Iain** *clambers to his feet.*

Please! Please no!

He stumbles and falls. He scrambles on the floor for the door. **Jay** *blocks the way.*

Iain   Please don't! Please don't kill me!

Jay   Listen –

Iain   I don't want to die! Not like this, please, not like this!

Jay   It's okay, just –

Iain   I have made many mistakes but I'll do whatever you want, just let me leave, and I'll be no trouble to you!

Jay   Shut up, Iain, you're freaking me out, I can't think!

Iain *whimpers, terrified.*

Iain   Please. Please.

Jay   Right. So. If we promise not kill you will you promise not to call the police?

Iain   Yes! Anything!

Jay   Okay. Then, uhh . . .

Zara   Shut up, Jay. We're not going to kill you, Iain, obviously. And he's not going to the fucking police. Look at him.

Iain *whimpers.*

Zara   I'll get you an ice pack.

Pause.

Iain   My life.

Zara   Yup.

Iain   All my life. My job. My wife.

Zara   I know.

Iain's *phone begins to ring. He looks around for it.* **Jay** *holds it up.*

Jay   It's her.

Beat.

She's not on Facebook, is she?

Iain   Course she is. It's all she ever does.

Jay   Right.

The phone continues to ring. **Jay** *holds the phone out.*

Do you want it?

Beat. **Iain** *shakes his head.*

Jay   Do you want me to answer it?

Beat. **Iain** *shrugs.*

Jay   What will I tell her?

Pause. **Iain** *shrugs. The phone rings.* **Jay** *answers.*

Jay   Hello. Yes, hi. This is Iain's phone, yes. My name is Jay and I am a male prostitute. Yes. That's correct. I have a message to pass on. From Iain. Um. He says, uh. He says . . . he says he's very sorry. You don't deserve this. You've done nothing wrong. But neither of you have been happy for a very long time.

Jay *looks over to* **Iain**, *who doesn't stop him.* **Jay** *continues.*

Jay   And he'd like to tell you, um. He'd also like to say that, uh –

Iain   Tell her it's going to be okay.

Jay   He says it's going to be okay.

Iain   She can have the house. She can sell it if she wants and live by the sea like she's always wanted.

Jay   He says you can have the house, if you want. And you should sell it and live by the sea like you've always wanted.

Iain   Tell her I hope she'll be freer this way. And she'll find some joy.

Jay   He says he hopes you'll be freer this way. And that you find –

Beat.

Jay   She's hung up.

Iain   Right.

Pause.

That's that then.

Pause.

That's that.

Pause. **Iain** *slumps back onto the bed. He stares a shell-shocked stare into the middle distance.* **Jay** *and* **Zara** *watch him, on edge, share a nervous glance, unsure of what the next move is.*

Zara   Fucking hell, Mr Urquhart.

Zara *watches as* **Iain** *retrieves his hip flask from earlier. He necks the remains. He tosses the flask aside.*

Iain   Woohoo.

Jay   What are you going to do now?

Iain   I have absolutely no idea.

Pause.

Zara   Right, fuck it. Jay, gimme my phone.

Jay   What?

Zara   My phone, give me it, you fanny!

Jay   You calling him?

Zara *nods. She dials.*

Jay   Put it on me, yeah? Like we said? You can sell this. Bullshit is your best shot.

She holds the phone up to her ear. It's ringing.

Zara   No.

Jay   What do you mean, no?

Zara   I'm sick of bullshit. Thanks anyway.

Jay   But we –

Zara   Don't worry. You'll still get your cash.

Jay   All of it?

Zara   All of it. (*Into phone.*) Dad. Yup. Uh huh. The picture. I've seen it yeah. I know. Yup. That's right. If I could . . . Uh huh. If I could just say . . . Dad. Dad. Dad. Dad, shut up for a minute. I'm going to talk to you about this. But first you need to have a little think. About whether you actually want to listen to me. And hear me. And if you do, you can call me back, whenever you've calmed down. And I'll be here. And if you don't, you can . . . you can, you can just go and fuck yourself. Okay? I love you. Bye.

Zara *tosses her phone away. She exhales.*

Jay   Jesus.

Beat.

Iain   I think that was very brave.

Zara   I don't actually need your approval, Iain, cheers though.

Iain   No. No, of course not.

Pause.

Iain   I'm going to put my trousers back on now.

Iain *picks up his clothes.*

This has been an extremely unusual afternoon. I'm going to leave now.

Iain *begins to get dressed.* **Jay** *looks to* **Zara***, unsure of what the next move is.* **Iain** *pulls on his trousers. He is still wearing the yellow shirt.*

Iain   This isn't mine.

Jay   Keep it, I suppose. As like a gesture. Or whatever.

Iain   Thanks.

Iain *heads towards the door, in search of his shoes.*

Zara   *The Lorax.*

Iain   Excuse me?

Zara   *The Lorax.* You ever read that one, to your kids?

Iain   Yes. Don't tell me. Dr Seuss was a Nazi or something, is that it?

Zara   Always weirdly reminded me of you, that book.

Iain   The one about the little hairy man who lives in trees?

Zara   Yeah. The ending. When the Once-ler guy gives the little boy the seed. Always did my head in that book.

Iain   Why?

Zara   Cos he's had it the whole fucking time, hasn't he?

Iain   Had what?

Zara   The seed. The last Truffula tree seed. He's had it in his own pocket the whole time. And this kid shows up and the Once-ler tells this big story about how he's cut down all the trees, and the land is barren, and how bad he feels about it. But now – now that the kid is here – the kid can, if he cares enough, can take the seed from him, and go and plant a new tree and make the world better again.

Iain It's a good message, isn't it?

Zara But why didn't he just plant the seed himself? He's looked at what a mess he's made of the world, and he's just sat there, with this seed in his pocket the whole time, and he's somehow convinced himself it's the kid's job to make it better. It's supposed to be an inspiring ending about the children being the future. But all he's done is avoid facing up to any of his own responsibility.

Iain I see. And that's why it reminded of you of me is it? I'm the Once-ler here, aren't I?

Zara I always thought that.

Beat.

Zara But, at some point you get older, and you have to accept that the world you're passing on is in a worse state than when you inherited it. And so, I wanted to say to you that, maybe I'm the Once-ler too. A bit. Maybe it's me too. I don't know.

Iain Well. In any case I am sorry.

Beat.

Zara Thank you. I'm sorry too. For . . . everything.

Iain I still think you've wilfully misinterpreted the spirit of the book.

Jay Book sounds shit anyway.

Iain And your little one, through there. What are you going to tell her? When she's older? Because things are going to get worse, aren't they? A lot worse.

Jay I don't know. I don't think like that.

Iain You're going to hope she doesn't blame her parents aren't you?

Jay   I'm just going to tell her that it's not her fault. That none of it is her fault. None of it. And so if she can just carry on, and live, and be her, and still just keep being her . . . then that, like, that's enough. That's more than enough for me. Sorry if that's not very inspiring.

Beat.

Iain   Beautiful.

Beat.

Where did you put my shoes? I should leave. Can I leave now?

Zara *and* **Jay** *look at each other.*

Zara   You can. If you want to.

Beat.

Or you can stay. And get what you paid for.

Jay   What?

Zara   You've still got twenty minutes on your clock. Right, Jay?

Jay   Uh . . . uh, fucking . . . yeah. I suppose. Yeah. Fair's fair.

Zara   It's a service, Iain. A paid for service. You might as well take it up.

Pause. Quietly, **Iain** *begins to cry.* **Zara** *nods for* **Jay** *to go to him. He does.* **Zara** *leaves.*

Jay   It's okay, Iain. Do you want – do you want me to hold you? Shall I hold you?

Blubbing, **Iain** *nods.* **Jay** *holds him.*

Jay   It's okay, Iain. It's okay.

Iain *cries.* **Jay** *leans his head on* **Iain**'s *shoulder.*

Jay   Do you want me to do this?

Crying, **Iain** *nods.*

Iain   I have been, all my life – so lonely . . .

Jay   Everyone's lonely.

Iain *nods.* **Jay** *caresses him, lovingly.*

Jay   It's okay. I know. I know. Me too. I know exactly how you feel.

Iain   You're just saying that. I can't tell if you're just saying that.

Jay *holds* **Iain** *close, intimately, like a lover.*

Jay   It doesn't matter. Do you want me to do this?

Iain *nods.*

Jay   Tell me what you want me to do.

Iain *lies down onto the floor.* **Jay** *cradles him.* **Iain** *cries.*

Jay   Like this?

Iain   Yes, this. Thank you.

Jay   Just this?

Iain   This. Yes. This.

Jay   Just this.

Iain   Just this.

Jay *holds* **Iain**. **Iain** *cries.*

The baby cries.

Blackout.